To Charlie,

With purrs and love.

Lua

The Book of Lua

Stories and wisdom from a little cat with mobility challenges

LUA & DANIA SHELDON

Kittenhaus Press

Editing by Gudrun Will
Photos by Dania Sheldon unless otherwise credited
Book design by Fiona Raven

First Printing, January 2018
Manufactured by Friesens in Canada

Library and Archives Canada Cataloguing in Publication

Lua (Cat), author
The book of Lua : stories and wisdom from a little cat with mobility challenges / by Lua and Dania Sheldon.

ISBN 978-0-9959039-0-6 (hardcover)

1. Lua (Cat)—Juvenile literature. 2. Cats—Biography—Juvenile literature. I. Sheldon, Dania, 1970–, author II. Title.

SF445.5.L83 2017 j636.80092'9
C2017-902714-X

Published by Kittenhaus Press
TheBookOfLua.com

FSC
www.fsc.org
MIX
Paper from responsible sources
FSC® C016245

To Bruce

My first friend.

To Mum and Dad

You took me into your home and hearts
when I was in greatest need of care and stability,
and you love me unconditionally
every single day.

To my cat buddies

You fill each day with friendship,
comfort, and the unexpected.

To my aunties and uncles and doctors

You brighten my days
with your messages and visits and love,
and you devote countless hours to rescuing
and helping other cats.

acknowledgements

Lua was born on 19 July 2013, and even before her first birthday, many people were asking for a book — about Lua's daily life and adventures, her challenges and triumphs, her friends and family, and her perspective as a cat with mobility challenges. I thank every one of you for your enthusiasm and encouragement.

The Book of Lua would not, though, have been remotely possible without the care, expertise, and wisdom of three individuals.

Martin Godwyn (aka Lua's dad) was resolutely supportive even when I was besieged with doubt. He also created many of the images and ensured that all of the photos and illustrations were of the highest possible quality for printing. Most of all, he provided love to the authors and the rest of their family.

Hinc lucem et pocula sacra.

Gudrun Will — long-time dear friend, exquisite writer, and meticulous editor — brought her tremendous blend of technical skills, wisdom, intuition, humour, and enthusiasm to the editing of the text. *The Book of Lua* is so much richer for her firm yet sensitive touch.

If the while I think on thee, dear friend,
All losses are restor'd and sorrows end.

Fiona Raven has made this a beautiful book. I have had the pleasure and privilege of working with Fiona for many years in a professional capacity. It was an honour and gift to have her bring the ideas, words, and images in *The Book of Lua* together in ways that I hadn't been able to imagine. As Keats wrote in "Endymion":

A thing of beauty is a joy forever:
Its loveliness increases; it will never
Pass into nothingness

I am also indebted to the brilliant author **A.L. Kennedy**, who has had nothing at all to do with *The Book of Lua*, but whose incredible writing has both discouraged and inspired me. I take heart from her blunt insights, such as this:

> *Write. No amount of self-inflicted misery, altered states, black pullovers or being publicly obnoxious will ever add up to your being a writer. Writers write. On you go.*

Dania
Gabriola Island
April 2017

Contents

Chapter 1

hello!

My name is Lua.

I also have nicknames, such as Kitten Face (which is kind of cute), Fluff Muffin (hmm, that makes me sound edible), Puffin (seriously, a bird?), Princess of Puff (better), and Fluff Butt (great, thanks a lot, Mum).

My preferred nickname is Principessa, which is from one of my mum's favourite films, *La Vita è Bella*; that's Italian for "Life Is Beautiful". The main character in that movie likes to greet his wife in the morning with the phrase, "Buongiorno, Principessa!" That's how Mum greets me each day.

But perhaps I should introduce myself a little bit more.

I live with my family on a small island called Gabriola, off the southwest coast of Canada.

I have a very happy life. Sometimes, it's a bit complicated. That's because I'm partially paralyzed, so I can't really stand up. And I definitely can't walk or jump, the way most cats can. But I can get to the top of a two-metre cat tower on my own, patrol our huge backyard, climb steep hills, scale our apple tree, and reach the second floor of our house to snuggle on the bed. And I can move so quickly in our meadows that my mum has to jog to keep up with me.

◂ *"Principessa"*

I decided to write this book because I realized that some people don't think I should be alive. They're not mean people, but they think that I can't be "a real cat", so I must be unhappy. Or they think that because I have to try harder to move around, I must be suffering. Or they find it upsetting to see me move around in an unusual way, differently from other cats.

Well, I can tell you — and I hope my book will make this clear — that I definitely enjoy being alive! Not being able to walk isn't the end of the world, even if you're a cat.

Happy to be alive!

I wasn't born paralyzed. When I was a very young kitten, I was in a bad accident that damaged a bunch of important nerves in the lower part of my spinal cord. Because I was so young, some of these nerves partially recovered, but other ones didn't.

My Auntie Karen, who helped me first after the accident, took me home and introduced me to Bruce, a big orange-and-cream cat with gentle eyes and soft paws.

Bruce had a terrible injury, too. He had been found homeless with a big wound around his neck that was still healing when I met him. We instantly knew that we had something in common and, even better, that we understood each other.

Bruce, my first friend

Bruce became my first friend, and he was amazing. He would play with me whenever I wanted, even when he was tired. He never got cross if I (accidentally) bit or scratched him when we were playing. I'm sure Bruce can growl and hiss, because all cats can, but I never heard him do that, ever.

He also kept me clean. Everybody knows that cats like to keep themselves *really* clean. I had trouble doing this, partly because I was so young, so I hadn't yet learned how to wash properly, and partly because my injury made it difficult for me to know when I needed to <ahem> use the litterbox.

He snuggled with me for naps and at bedtime. I never felt alone or worried when I was with Bruce.

In those early weeks after the accident, I went to see doctors a lot. *A lot.* Poke. Prod. Squeeze. I had acupuncture. And water therapy — that was really scary! And on and on and on. The doctors weren't sure how much I would recover.

Auntie Karen is a very busy person because she spends every single day rescuing cats. She decided that I needed someone who could look after me more, supervise me, take me to a bazillion medical appointments, and give me physical therapy. There were just too many other cats she needed to help.

Bruce was always close by

Unfortunately, this meant saying goodbye to Bruce, at least for a while. He needed a different kind of home. We touched noses, and he gave my forehead a last lick — "For old time's sake," he said. I felt sure that I would see him again, so I didn't cry.

That is how I moved to Gabriola Island.

Chapter 2

daily life

I've had quite a few people ask me what my daily life is like, so I'll try to describe a more or less typical day.

My home is a three-storey house located in the middle of meadows and forest. Our property is about the size of six football fields! For a small cat like me, this is quite big and exciting. On days when the weather is really bad, I climb the stairs or the cat trees inside the house, but otherwise, I go outside whenever possible.

I'm an early riser, so when Mum (also an early riser) comes downstairs in the morning, I'm usually already awake. At home, I sleep in my own room. This is to keep me safe overnight from one of the cats, Lord Grey, who sometimes tries to ambush me. It's nothing personal; he tries to do this to several of the other cats, too, but they're better able to defend themselves or run away. (Mum feels bad that he's like this and has asked him to stop, but he doesn't seem able to control himself. It might be because he used to be feral, which means "almost wild".)

Once Mum opens the door to my room, I say good morning, then do some stretches. My back can get pretty sore, so stretching throughout the day is important.

◂ *Relaxation is an important part of daily life*

I like to stretch

Exercise helps keep me healthy

Then it's time for The First Squeeze of the Day. Since I can't stand up to use the litter box, Mum has to "express" my bladder three or four times a day to help me stay clean and healthy. I don't like this. She has to hold onto me and squeeze quite firmly on my bladder to push out the urine. Even though we've done this hundreds of times, I still hate it, and Mum feels bad about that. I try not to show my annoyance — and sometimes, I succeed! Other times, I'm cranky and protest by growling or by biting or scratching her. (Sorry, Mum.) She gets it done so quickly, though.

Breakfast is next, but I'm usually not very interested. If I were a human, I would probably have just toast and coffee in the morning! If I'm feeling hungry, I'll have a small amount of tuna, or some raw beef, or some canned food. I think it's good that I'm not a big eater, because if I weighed more, it would be harder for me to move around. In case you're wondering, I weigh about eight pounds, or three and a half kilograms. My doctors say this is a perfect weight for me.

Usually, the first thing I want to do is go outside. I make a beeline for the back door and wait for Mum to open it. Then — zoom! I launch myself out onto the deck and find out what the weather is like.

The region of the world where I live is called a "temperate rainforest"; as you can imagine, it rains a lot. Sometimes it even snows! I've had to figure out strategies for these days. Most often, I'll sit for a while, sniffing the air and gauging how wet I might get if I go any further. My fur is *very* long, so once it gets wet, it takes ages to dry. Mum always puts a chair and blankets in a sheltered spot outside the back door, and I often decide to sit there, hearing the morning news from the birds and checking the skies.

Dawn

When it isn't raining or really cold, I scoot across the back deck, stop at the edge of the stairs to make sure everything looks safe, then hurry down to the yard — bump, bump, bump, bump!

It's time for the first patrol of the day, initially under the deck, then out into the rest of the yard. This part slopes down to the fence, so making my way around gives me a good workout because afterward, I climb back up the slope on my own. Mum offers to help, but I'm what you'd call "very independent"; I like to do things myself if I possibly can.

Many deer live around our home. If any of them are nearby, I'll often go and chat with them for a bit. When we first met, I think they were puzzled because I don't move the way the other cats do. After I explained, they just nodded and asked whether I was happy. "Yes," I replied, "I'm very happy most of the time. Are you?"

The deer nodded again, and one of them, named Galahad, said, "Most of the time. This land where you and the other cats and your mum and dad live is very safe for us. No dogs chase us, and no one hunts us, and the vegetation is lush, and the water is fresh and clean, and we can lie down

Some of my deer friends

Galahad

in the meadows or near the house without worrying. These are all good things that make us happy."

Many days, I like to go out to The Mouse Garden. This is another fenced area, just across from the yard. It contains a cherry tree, an apple tree, a tiny oak tree, a mulberry bush, and several raspberry bushes, plus lots of grass and flowers. And *many* mice! I call it The Mouse Garden because it seems like this is where mice grow.

Aside from checking on what the mice are doing, I dig in the dirt — not where the mouse holes are, but in a few different spots, just for fun. My upper body is particularly strong, and I find it invigorating to dig like crazy. If Mum isn't in the garden with me, I'll sometimes call to her so she can come out to admire my latest holes. I take her on a little tour, showing her one, demonstrating my digging skills at another, and then tearing off into the grass so she'll follow me. Although I'm independent, I do like her company sometimes.

On warm, sunny days, Mum sometimes takes a blanket and her computer into the garden to work there. She always brings me water and a snack, too. If I get sleepy, I doze off near her; every so often, we doze off together.

◂ *Taking a break from digging*

Climbing the stairs

On the big cat tower

If the day really is too wet or cold to be outside, I hang out indoors, either in front of the wood stove, or on one of the cat towers (which I climb by myself), or in my red tube, which is made of fabric and is about three times longer than me, even if I stretch out my tail!

If I feel like it, I climb the stairs to the second floor and visit with the cats up there.

Grooming takes up quite a bit of time, because my fur is thick as well as long.

Occasionally, one of my aunties will come over to play with and brush me. These are ladies who love cats and got to know me when I first came to live on Gabriola. They're busy people, so when they have time to hang out, I really appreciate it.

Unless it's too cold or wet, I'll be outside until dusk, then come indoors. There's a floor-to-ceiling cat tower in the living room, and sometimes I'll scare Mum by climbing up to the very top along the least safe route. I think she worries too much — but she says worrying is part of her job.

When it's time for me to go to bed, I usually dash into the red tube and wait to be carried from the living room to "my" room. Mum and Dad call this "taking The Tube" because Dad is from London and Mum has spent quite a bit of time there, too. When Dad's home, he picks one of the 270 London Underground stations as my destination for the night, and then off I go.

RAVENSCOURT PARK

Mind the gap!

I love my Magic Bag

Mum always warms up a Magic Bag for me, in case I feel like lying on that. It's made of cotton cloth and filled with oat grains, and after being warmed up

in a microwave, it gives off heat for an hour. It's really soothing for my muscles and joints.

She makes sure I have fresh water and a plate of food in case I get the munchies. Then she gives me a few treats, kisses and snuggles me a bit, and closes the door to keep me safe. Some nights, one or two of my best cat buddies, Pedro and Bear and Mouse, will stay in the room with me. We play tag, tell each other stories, snooze, watch the night life out the big windows (raccoons, the occasional deer, and sometimes a cat from another home in the neighbourhood), tidy up our fur and nails, doze some more . . . and in no time, it's morning again.

It's morning again!

In my dreams, sometimes I can fly!

Chapter 3

the great outdoors

For the first couple of months after I moved to Gabriola, I stayed indoors. I had several infections, and it just wasn't a good idea for me to go outside — or even beyond my upstairs room — most of the time. Mum spent at least eight hours a day in that room, playing with me and making sure I had snuggles when I needed them. And I had visits from some of the other cats as well as my aunties.

Finally, I was healthy enough to have my first outdoor experience, although I didn't know anything yet about the great wide world that I would get completely hooked on. It was December. In Canada, that's wintertime, and winter sometimes means snow.

Wow! My first experience of the outside world was . . . WHITE. Pretty much everywhere.

Moving through snow was challenging for me. I tried to pull myself along with my front legs, but I couldn't get a good grip. Also, if I sank down, I couldn't jump out again. So, Mum created paths for me, and I explored this strange, amazing, big world.

Mum decided to film me during my first experience of snowflakes falling. One of my uncles then found the perfect song for the video and posted it on YouTube. (At the back of this book, on page 97, I've

◂ *What's all this white stuff?*

I can do this . . .

Wow, it's deep!

put website addresses for this video and several others.)

There were so many new sounds and smells! Big black creatures passed overhead, and at first, I was scared of them. But I soon learned that they were ravens, and that this was their home, too. In fact, we became friends (at a comfortable distance). Now, they help me keep track of what's going on in our yard and meadows.

I was so fascinated by the whiteness that I actually didn't notice the cold until I started to shiver. Mum then scooped me up in a fluffy towel and placed me on a blanket in front of the wood stove, where a fire was burning. I hadn't ever seen a fire before. Like the ravens, it was a bit scary at first. Then I felt the warmth, and my fur began to dry and fluff up, and . . . I drifted off to sleep.

That day was quite an adventure!

Although snow is pretty and can be fun to a certain extent, it is also a bit . . . monotonous. White, white, white, and it covers up a lot of interesting things. Mouse holes, for example.

Of course, in that first winter, I didn't know anything about mouse holes or mice, so I was happy burrowing around in the snow. It was great to get out of the house and build up my strength. There were even a lot of birds. Mum maintains nine feeders for the hummingbirds all year round, so those tiny creatures were some of my first bird friends. Yes, cats and birds can be friends!

My friend Anna

My first spring

When the snow melted and the rains eased up, I experienced my first spring. What a thrill! Everything was growing, including me.

Mum started to take me on longer and longer walks. First, these were just inside the yard closest to the house, which is surrounded by special fencing to keep us cats safe. Then, we went into The Mouse Garden.

Being a cat, I find it pretty much irresistible to try to locate and catch mice. I soon discovered that I could enjoy being in The Mouse Garden for hours at a time, checking on the many mouse holes, sniffing for the latest whereabouts of the occupants, and listening for the faint pattering of their tiny feet along the ground, the scratching of their claws in the dirt.

At first, I thought that when I found one and started playing with it, Mum would run into the garden to join us. But Mum doesn't share my views about mice. I soon realized that she was trying to get the mouse away from me, and this was a cause for some disagreement! Now, I try not to let her know when I've found a mouse to play with.

Some days, the mice were not around, so I climbed the apple tree. This gave me an excellent view above the grass, and I realized that there was a much bigger fenced area beyond The Mouse Garden. Soon, I learned this was The Hummingbird Garden. And it needed exploring, too.

The Hummingbird Garden contains the feeders for the hummingbirds. It's at least six times bigger than The Mouse Garden and has a lot of little hills and paths. So, it's a great place to get exercise — and to hide from Mum. In the summertime, when the grass grows to over a metre high, I can disappear. Then I sometimes stay very, very still, because I like to pretend I'm a lion in the savannah: big and powerful and stealthy. Mum has shown me photos and videos of lions in Africa, and she says that I'm distantly related to them. Wow!

Prowling in the grass

One of my relatives!

◂ *Climbing the apple tree*

Spending time in the gardens and meadows has helped me get to know so many of the animals who live out there all the time and who call our little piece of land home, too.

Basically, I live in a beautiful park, and I love it.

Our beautiful park ▸

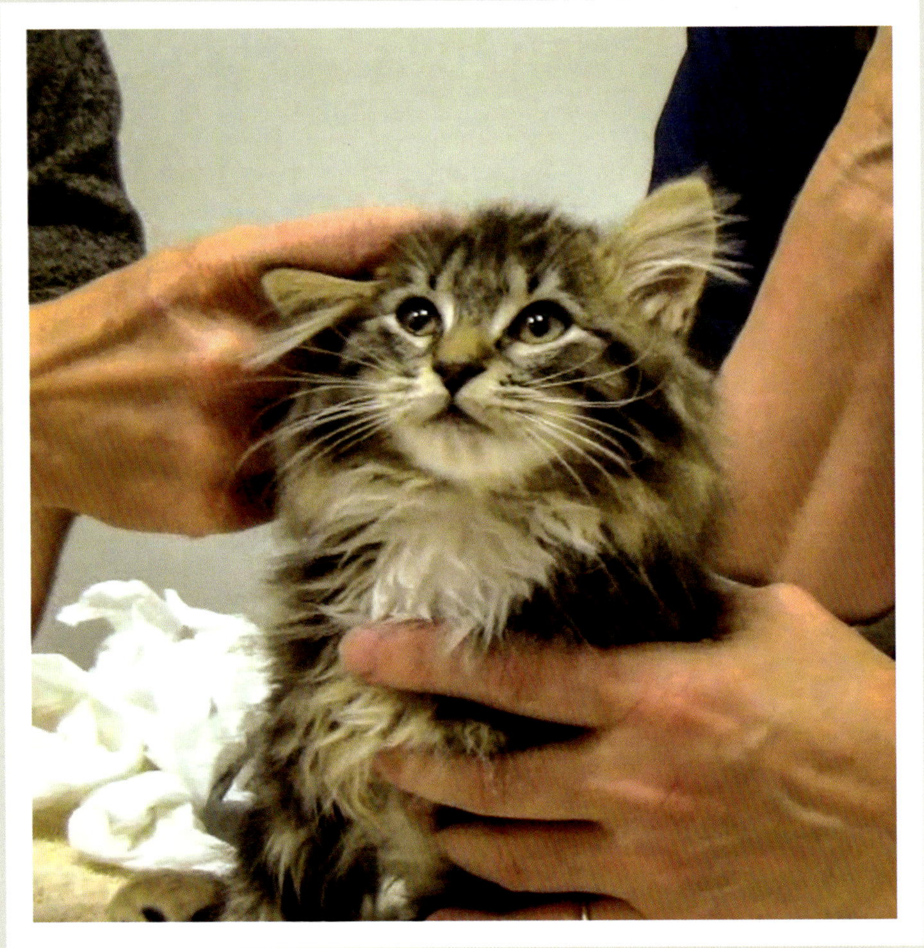

Chapter 4

doctors & medicine

I don't always get to explore the gardens surrounding my home. Sometimes, because of my health issues, the plan for my day is a trip to the doctor — yuck. I don't mean that the doctor is yucky, it's just that I don't much enjoy getting poked and prodded. Who does? And it's usually a long journey to get there and back home. Often, I need to take medicine afterwards for many days in a row.

If you've ever been sick and had to see a doctor — and I bet every single one of you reading this has had that experience, maybe only a few times, or maybe many, many times, like me — you know that it's not fun. Sure, it's good to get help. But when I'm sick, I also just want to hide under a blanket and be left alone. We don't always have that choice.

An early visit to the doctors

Right after my accident, I saw a lot of Dr. Sue and Dr. Janice, two veterinarians (animal doctors) who work together. I call them Auntie Sue and Auntie Janice. They're super special because they help keep me healthy, and they give Mum so much support, especially when she's worried about me. One of the many reasons we love them is because they're honest and straightforward. They "tell it like it is", even when the news isn't pleasant.

At first, Dr. Sue said that things weren't looking too good for my future. I had a lot of infections. Plus, Mum was on a steep learning curve, trying to get to know me and figure out how to do difficult things such as squeeze out my bladder. She also had to give me half baths twice a day until I could keep myself clean. Like a lot of cats, I hate water, so I was terrified during every bath. I would cry, and so would Mum. It was not a happy time for us.

However, I'm quite determined, and so is Mum, and so are Auntie Janice and Auntie Sue.

For several months, I also went to see Dr. Charoul, who works in a small town on Vancouver Island. I would visit her every couple of weeks for therapy — maybe acupuncture, or laser, or physiotherapy, or all three. It was hard for Mum to take so much time off work, so one of my Gabriola aunties would usually take me to see Dr. Charoul. The ferry and car rides were long, but I would come back feeling all "Zen" after treatment sessions.

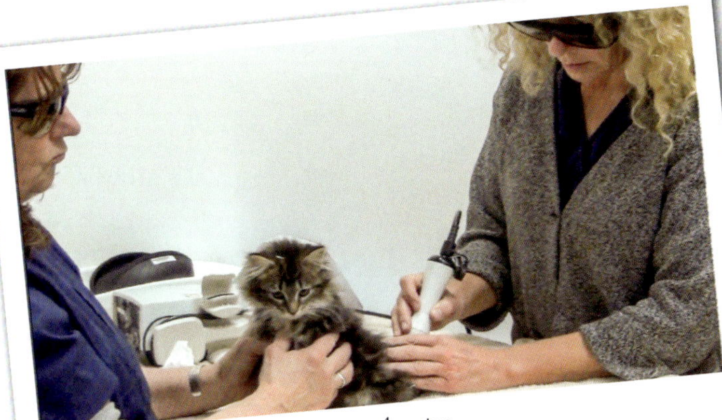

Laser therapy

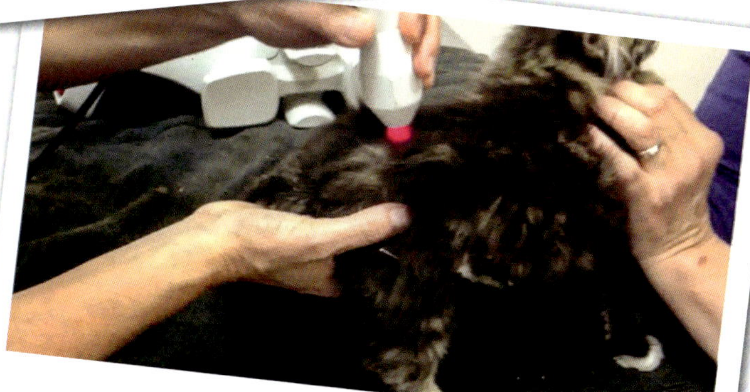

It didn't hurt

Acupuncture

▲ *Feeling "Zen" after therapy*

At one point, I had a particularly nasty skin infection that was scarier for Mum than for me because I couldn't see it, or even feel it very much. We got help from Dr. Trish on Gabriola, who was really gentle and helped me recover. I took some medicine called an antibiotic, and Mum spent many hours for the next couple of weeks keeping the infected area clean until new skin grew and I was totally better.

In that early time, I was taking medicine pretty much every day, which is just icky, so I would try to spit it out. More arguments with Mum. More tears. But I tried to cooperate. Slowly, with the help of all four doctors, my condition started to improve.

Then the news came from Auntie Janice: I would not walk again.

She's a rehabilitation specialist, which means that she knows a lot about how to help cats and dogs who have mobility challenges. In fact, Auntie Janice lives with a dog who has rear-leg paralysis, like me. We'd hoped that I might relearn to walk with my back legs. I can kick them, and I can lift my tail a bit and swish it around. I definitely have some sensation from my mid-back down to my back toes and my tail. But it seems that my brain and the nerves and muscles there don't quite know how to talk to each other properly. So, Auntie Janice said, I needed to prepare for a life of limited mobility. I think this news was harder on Mum than it was on me.

One of my aunties purchased a custom-made cart for me; I could be strapped into it, and then I would move with my front legs, and the wheels at the back would help me get around quickly. I absolutely hated it. I felt really bad about this, but the straps and the cart hurt. Auntie Janice said that because I have feeling in my lower back and my back legs, the cart was bothering me rather than helping. Fortunately, another cat got to use the cart instead of me, and Mum says it helped her.

I'm pretty sure that I can remember a time when I could walk. But since then, I've simply been living in the body that I have. I've learned how to move around quickly enough, and I can climb and explore almost anywhere I want. I play with the other cats. I keep myself clean (no more baths!). I chase insects and mice (even though Mum wishes I wouldn't). Of course, sometimes I look at the other cats and wish I could leap the way they can, run the way they can, stand up the way they can. But that's the way it is. With the help of my doctors, and Mum and Dad, and our friends, I've figured out a happy way of living.

Chapter 5

dragons

Let's get back to the outdoors so that I can tell you about one of my passions: watching for dragons.

It was the ravens and bald eagles who first educated me about dragons. Ravens and eagles can fly very high, soaring upwards on columns of rising air and gaining amazing views of the earth below. That high up, they can spot dragons from a great distance.

You might have been told that dragons don't exist. That's simply not true. Most humans can't see dragons, which is why that belief is common. But the fact that you can't see something doesn't mean it's not there. We can't see air, for example, but we need it to stay alive.

Alert!

I will state here, for the record: Dragons exist.

Dragons aren't all the same. In fact, they have as many different personalities as humans or cats do. For example, they can be really scary — breathing fire and scorching the treetops, roaring as they swoop through

◂ *A giant snow dragon*

the air, and chasing little creatures (including cats). Or they can be quiet, shy, gentle, and kind, giving a protective wing to migrating birds who are too tired to reach a safe resting place for the night.

How dragons behave usually depends on how they're treated. I learned this from the little brown bats who live in our house. They know all the dragons who either visit or live on Gabriola Island. Unlike most of the birds, who tend to be afraid of the dragons, the bats are friendly with them, even with the scariest ones.

When the bats told me about the dragons, I was a bit concerned. Dragons are huge! Many of them are a lot bigger than the house where

Little brown bats ▸

I live, and some of them have wingspans as large as a 747 airplane. Even baby dragons (who are incredibly cute) can be six times bigger than I am.

"What should I do?" I asked the bats. "How can I enjoy going outside now, knowing that dragons could be lurking to swoop down and get me at any moment?"

The bats laughed (very kindly). "Lua," said the smallest one, "it's simple: make friends with them."

"But how?" I asked. "They're huge, and I'm very, very small, and they might eat me before I can even open my mouth to speak!"

"Just be yourself," said the biggest bat.

"How can I be anyone *except* myself?" I asked.

"That's a good point," replied the middle-sized bat, chuckling. "What we mean, though, is *be who you would be if nobody else were there*. No person is completely herself when she's with

A baby dragon

someone else. When we're with other people, we need to play a role. Think about it. When we're with our parents, we play the role of the child. When we're with friends, we play the role of the friend we think we should be. When we're being taught in school (bats go to school, too, you know), we play the role of the student. There's nothing wrong with playing roles. If we didn't do this, we wouldn't be able to live together peacefully, because everyone has many different ideas about how we should co-exist. We need to cooperate. And to cooperate, we need to play different roles. Every role I play is a part of who I am. Every role that *you* play is a part of who *you* are."

I thought about this for quite a while. Then I said, "So, you're saying that with the dragons, I should be the person I would be if I were totally by myself. But how can I do that if I'm with a dragon? I wouldn't be by myself!"

The smallest bat, who had started this discussion, said, "Hmmm, that's a good point. Well, how about being as close to your me-by-myself person as you can?"

"I think I can do that," I said.

So, I started my first Dragon Patrol. I admit that initially, all I wanted was to keep our home safe from the dangerous dragons. But I kept talking with the bats. And as the days and weeks and months went by, I tried more and more to let the dragons know that I wanted to be their friend.

One day, I had an amazing and important encounter.

It was a sunny day, and the sky was incredibly blue, without a single cloud. Then, seemingly from nowhere, a trio of dragons swooped down and perched just a few feet away from me.

The biggest dragon breathed flames right over my head. That was awfully scary! But once I recovered, I realized that she didn't mean harm, otherwise she could have done much worse. Instead, she looked over at the other dragons and seemed to be waiting for instructions.

The dragon trio

She had impressive wings

The smallest dragon laughed at me. "Silly kitten! Don't you know that dragons and cats are natural enemies? You'll come to a bad end, you know!" Yet although he rose up and swooped close, he didn't breathe any fire toward me at all. In fact, he seemed a little nervous or uncomfortable.

The middle-sized dragon flew very close; I could feel the air from the beating of her impressive wings. "Little cat, why are you doing this?" she asked softly. "Don't you know that you might be eaten at any moment, or burnt to a crisp? I'm gentle, but many dragons aren't. You'd be much safer if you accepted that cats and dragons aren't supposed to be friends."

I was confused.

"If you're all dragons, why do you behave so differently? Why do some of you want to eat me, others to scare me, and others to protect me? I don't understand!"

The dragons stopped. They were silent and seemed perplexed.

The biggest dragon spoke. "I don't know. This is what I was taught to do." She looked down, seeming embarrassed. "I guess I'm not sure how else to behave . . ."

The smallest dragon leaned over against the big one and said, "I was taught to be like that, too. Except one day, I made friends with a kitten. My family didn't approve, so I had to give up our friendship, but I've never forgotten her. I guess you, little cat, remind me of her a bit."

The medium dragon said, "My parents died very soon after I was born. They were gentle dragons, but a human who didn't know that killed them with a bow and arrows. I was very small and completely alone. That night, a mother cat found me. I thought she would kill me, but instead, she took me softly in her mouth and carried me back to her nest, where there were four black kittens, identical to their momma. She curled around us, and I grew up as part of a cat family."

The momma cat

The other two dragons looked at her, and the big one said, "I never knew that!"

She replied, "You never asked."

There was a slightly awkward silence, and I cleared my throat.

"Um, I'm not sure whether you know this already," I said, "but my name is Lua. This is my home, and I live here with my mum and my dad and a few other cats. And if you think you can be nice to me and to all of them, then you're welcome to stay."

▾ *They decided to stay*

These three dragons did decide to stay, and they've become part of our family. However, there are still a lot of unhappy, angry, aggressive dragons out there, so we have to remain vigilant. I wish this weren't the case. But the truth is that I have to do Dragon Patrol pretty much every day, so that the birds and bats and I can keep track of what dragons are nearby. I'd like them all to become friends, but you can't make someone do that. Friendship is something that only happens by choice.

Chapter 6

friends & family

Friends and family are very important.

I'm not what you'd call really sociable. I do like company if I'm in the right mood. However, I also like to be on my own a lot. And as I've mentioned earlier, I prefer to try things on my own instead of getting help. There are days when I spend hours alone out in The Mouse Garden, exploring the paths and investigating mouse holes and listening to the sounds of nature. And I'm very happy doing that.

But even those of us who are solitary types enjoy and need the company of good friends and family sometimes. These are people we can trust, no matter what. Who will listen to us whether we're happy or sad. Who will understand if we act like a jerk sometimes but don't really mean to. Who will accept our apology and say, "It's OK, I'll always love you."

Me and my friend Zeb

Sometimes, a stuffed animal can be our friend.

◀ *Friends can relax together*

Something I've come to realize is that it's not important how many friends you have. But it's very important that they're kind and sincere and honest with you.

Where I live now, my best friends are Mouse, Pedro, and Bear. Mouse and I look so much alike that you might think we were sisters, or that she's my cat mum.

Mouse makes me laugh. She really doesn't like any of the other cats, and she grumbles about them to me in private. But for some reason, Mouse decided I'm OK. ("Maybe you look like the little sister I never had," she once admitted.) We hang out quite a bit, especially in the colder months, when there's a fire in the wood stove and we bask in front of it together.

Mouse

Pedro and Bear are really mellow. They've lived with Mum since they were two days old. She bottle-fed them because they were taken away from their cat mum shortly after being born (very sad for them and for her), and they've hung out with me ever since

I came to live here. They don't groom me, the way Bruce used to, but that's because I told them I'm fine to take care of it on my own.

Bear is a good buddy to Stellar, too. He's lying on top of Bear in this photo.

Stellar is a bit like me because he also has some mobility challenges. He was born with something called cerebellar hypoplasia, which means that although he can stand up and walk, he wobbles and falls over a lot. Sometimes, we talk about what it's like to move differently than the other cats. Like me, he's very comfortable with who he is, and he's incredibly strong, too!

Another of my cat friends is Curly. He's exceedingly wise and has taught me a lot of things. I really

Pedro

Stellar and Bear

look up to him. But when he's not in the mood to be sociable, he tells me — politely but directly — and I give him his space. I'm just as straightforward with him. We're totally honest with each other.

I appreciate that we can be in the same area for hours at a time, not talking about anything and just being ourselves. Sometimes, he comes out into The Hummingbird Garden with me and Mum, and that's fantastic, because he tells me all about the different plants and birds. He keeps an eye on me so that I don't wander too far from Mum, but he also lets me sneak away sometimes, just to tease her. Curly always knows where I am, though. True friends have your back even when you're being mischievous or foolish.

Curly

Some friends I haven't yet met in person, because we've gotten to know each other using the Internet. They look at the photos I post, and they send me messages. Sometimes, they send me packages in the mail, with catnip and toys and other neat stuff. It's so exciting when a parcel arrives!

With Mum's help, I always send them a note of thanks and photos of me with the presents, so they know how much I appreciate their thoughtfulness.

A few of these friends have come to visit us on Gabriola, and that's really neat, too. I get to show them around the house, then out in the yard, and then out in The Mouse Garden. If the weather is good, I demonstrate my digging and climbing skills, and we laugh a lot. I love sharing our home and meadows and forests with my friends and family.

I'm very lucky to have amazing, loving cats and humans in my life. I've told you about Bruce, whom I hope to meet again someday soon. Well, just as I was finishing writing this book, he sent me an email! Here's what he wrote:

Dear Lua,

Hi there, it's me, Bruce! It's been quite a long time since we said goodbye at Auntie Karen's house, so I thought I would send you a note, especially as my mum tells me that you're publishing a book. Wow! That's so exciting.

I now have a house with a nice yard filled with birds and other cats, whom I watch through big windows, and I'm really happy here. My family is

Bruce at his cottage

Bruce and his dad

awesome. Would you like to visit us one day? I know you live on Gabriola Island now, but Mum says you come over to the mainland quite often. Or better yet, come see me on Salt Spring Island, as I now have a cottage there, too. Mum lets me outside there sometimes. You could watch me climb trees! Mum says I'm "getting my CAT back" when I do that. It would be great to see you again!

Lots of love,

Bruce (my family calls me Brew sometimes, but mostly Mr. Kitty, but I will always be Bruce with you)

P.S. I've attached a couple of recent photos.

I think that if we make sure to tell our friends and family how much we appreciate them, we'll all have happier lives. It sounds simple — because it is. Don't be embarrassed. Tell them, "Hey, you know what? You're awesome, and I'm really glad you're in my life. Thank you." We cats do it all the time. It's that easy, and I promise you won't regret it.

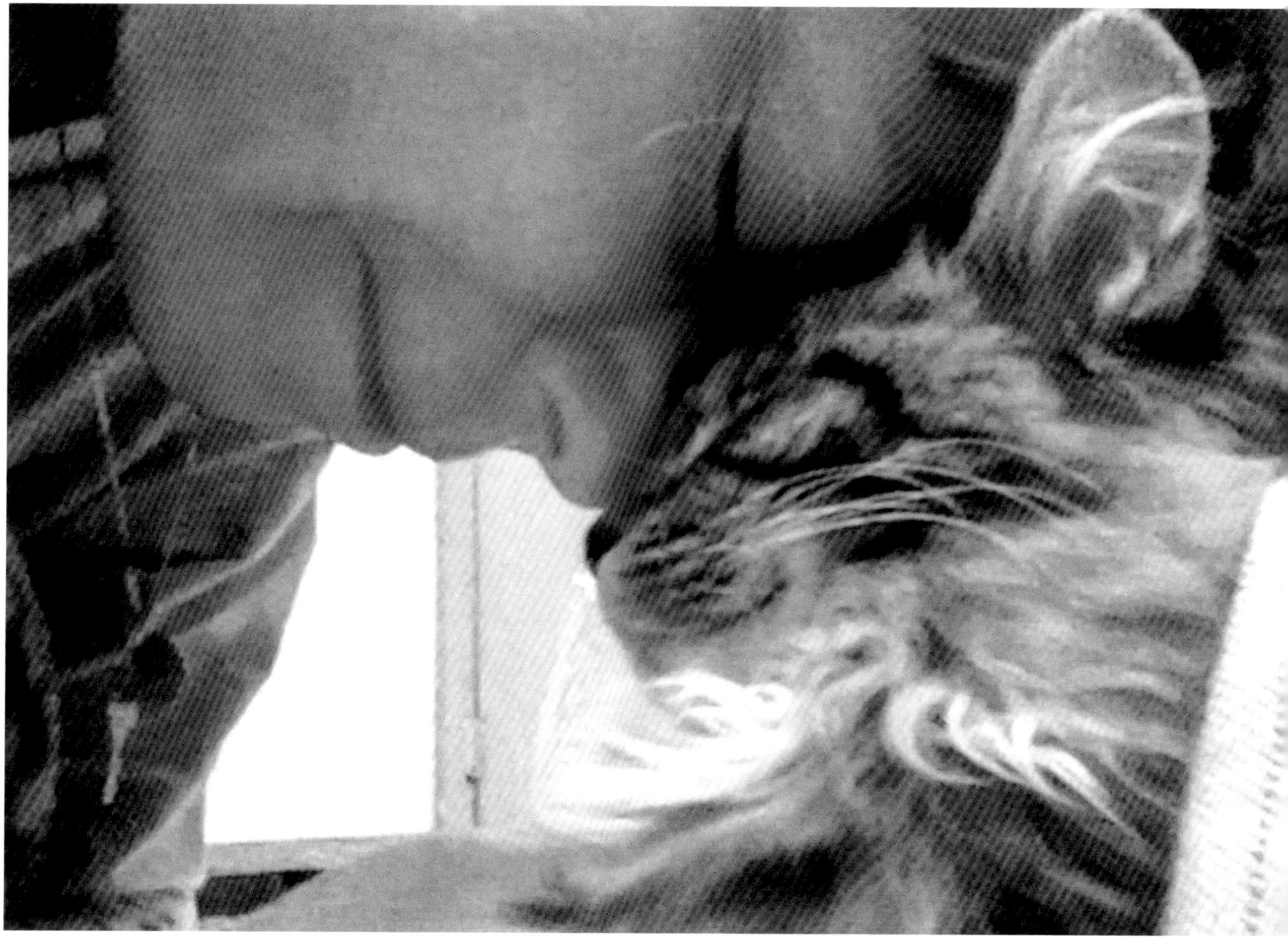

▲ *"I love you."*

Chapter 7

helping other folks

Once I had befriended the dragons, we started spending time together in The Mouse Garden and beyond. The dragons feel more comfortable there than near the house, since I haven't yet convinced all of the other cats that dragons and cats can be friends.

The dragons and I like to wander and explore. Occasionally, during these explorations, I discover someone who needs help. Last summer, Mum was searching for me in the very long grass. She couldn't find me, so she walked through the yard in places where she doesn't usually walk. That's how she found me sitting near a tiny bat, who was on the ground in broad daylight. I had checked with my dragon friends, and they'd said that no bat would want to be in that position. I then had asked the bat, and she'd said, "I definitely don't want to be here. I'm scared, but I feel too weak and confused to get off the ground."

I couldn't help her, so I was waiting for Mum to find us both. She immediately scooped up my new bat friend (BF) and spent the rest of that day looking after BF, hoping for her recovery. Mum was very worried, so I asked why she was trying so hard to save this bat.

She explained that she believes all creatures should be valued. She also told me that bats are having a very hard time right now because

▲ *A tiny pipistrelle bat*

of a disease called White-nose Syndrome. This is causing bats to die in large numbers throughout North America. Bats, she said, are an important part of our ecosystems, because they help to keep a whole bunch of natural cycles in balance. For example, little brown bats can eat 600 insects in an hour, sometimes much more than that. Insects are also important, but it's better for everyone if there aren't too many of them.

While Mum was looking after BF, I asked the dragons what they knew about bats. I learned that bats and dragons have a lot in common. Bats, like dragons, are very unusual because they fly but don't have feathers; bats have fur, like me. Dragons have scales (the way fish and snakes do). Also, a lot of people don't like bats or dragons, which is unfortunate, in my opinion. Another thing is that some bats are very social, living in huge colonies of more than a million, like humans in cities. Other bats, like the ones who live at our house, prefer quieter, more solitary lives and just hang out with their family and close friends; dragons are the same.

I'm a lot like shy, quiet bats and dragons. I enjoy the company of Mum and Dad and the other cats — until I don't.

We have two bat houses attached to our home, and a few little brown bats have been living in those houses and in our rafters for a long time. Little brown bats can live for many years — at least six, and in at least one case up to thirty-one. So, it's possible that some of these bats have been here longer than Mum and Dad. Bat babies are called pups, and bats usually have one pup a year, sometimes twins.

Mum saves even the tiniest of flies, so I know that she'll try to save anyone. (She has saved many mice from me — maybe we shouldn't talk about that here, because mice are related to bats.) Anyway, I was really intrigued about her dedication to this little bat. She helped BF hang upside down in a box. I asked why BF would want to hang upside down. (I find that really uncomfortable!) She explained that bats rest and sleep this way, because it takes very little effort, and they're so small that their blood doesn't rush to their heads the way it does in larger mammals.

Later, I talked with my dragon friends, and they said they often do this, too (depending on whether they're small that day or not — dragons can change size according to their mood). Sometimes, other folks are a lot more different and interesting than you realize!

But let's get back to BF. Because bats are nocturnal, Mum knew that it would be important for BF to be outdoors, hopefully within hearing of family members, as dusk began to fall. So, she took BF to a nearby and very safe branch, then gently helped her hang upside down.

As the light diminished, BF started waking up more and looking around, including at us. We decided it would be best to go away, so that BF and her family could feel comfortable.

When we went back in half an hour, BF was gone — and there were three bats flying through the night air!

Our bat friend, BF

We felt so glad. And as I looked out at The Mouse Garden, I could see three sets of glowing eyes. My dragon friends were very happy that BF was going to be OK.

This was an excellent day. Now, when the bats fly around in the evening, I think about the importance of friendship, and living together peacefully, and helping one another. I look up and say, "Hello! I'm glad you live here, too."

That's how I feel about all of the folks Mum has helped over the years: bats, snakes, salamanders, frogs, beetles, moths, snails, slugs, birds, and so many others. This place is home for all of us.

Chapter 8

magic

Are dragons magical? Can cats be magical? Can you be magical? Does magic even exist?

I think it does. I believe we're surrounded by magic, in many, many forms. But we need to use our hearts to find it.

Personally, I believe magic is part of anything and anyone that makes us truly, deeply happy inside. I don't mean things such as food (although I do enjoy treats) or catnip (which is a lot of fun). Those are things that make me happy for a short while. But my heart doesn't glow from food or catnip.

Magic, for me, is being outdoors, enjoying the world. Listening to what the birds and bats and dragons and insects are saying, what the grasses whisper to me, the chiming of the columbine bells (which is very, very quiet, but if you listen very, very carefully, you can hear it).

Columbine bells

◀ *Magic exists!*

Magic, for me, is also being indoors, enjoying the love and friendship of my family.

Mum thinks my toe floofs are magical!

Seemingly ordinary things can actually be magical. For example, Mum sometimes wears a piece of clothing that she calls a bathrobe. But to me, and to many of the other cats in my family, it's "The Magic Robe". It doesn't do anything amazing — it doesn't fly through the air, for example. But it provides the most wonderful comfort. Whenever I step onto it, I suddenly become so relaxed. The same happens to the other cats. Without us even realizing it, our paws start kneading the soft, squishy fabric, our eyes half close, we begin purring, we go into a kind of trance, and we drift into another place . . .

Mum thinks that maybe the robe reminds us of when we were kittens,

◂ *Magic is all around us*

cuddled up against our cat momma, kneading her soft belly. But four of the cats were orphaned right after they were born, so they never got to know their cat momma at all, yet they still respond the same way to The Magic Robe.

I asked my dragon friends what they think about magic, whether it exists. One of them snorted (which was a bit dangerous, because fire came out of his nose, but I managed to jump out of the way — he apologized).

"Of course it exists! We wouldn't be here without magic. And besides, the ordinary world can be very sad sometimes. We all need magic to remind us that happiness and beauty are always close at hand, even if they're sometimes tough to find. That's what magic is for, to help us find them."

I don't believe in a magic that will cure me of my paralysis. I'm a practical cat, and I don't think miracles occur. And it would take a miracle to make me walk again. But I do think that humans sometimes forget about how important magic is in our everyday lives. The sound of the breeze through leaves — that's magic. The humming of bees in a flower patch — that's magic. The migration of my friends the rufous hummingbirds, who every year fly the length of an entire continent to

He snorted ▸

Mexico, and then back again in the spring — that's magic. Me making friends with the bats and the dragons — that's magic.

Many adults think that it's childish to believe in magic. I disagree. Of course magic exists. It's all around us, all the time.

Befriend a dragon!

My magic sleeping circle ▸

Chapter 9

journeys

By the time this book is published, I'll be four years old. Cats can live to be over twenty, so if everything goes well for me, I'll be only one-fifth of the way through my big journey in this world.

I've already had several smaller journeys — my injury, meeting and being taken care of by Bruce, moving to Gabriola, discovering the outdoors and dragons and bats and birds and deer, being nurtured by vets and aunties and Mum and my cat buddies, building and testing my strength as I learned to adapt to my physical challenges, realizing the value of patience (and sometimes forgetting it, too).

I've figured out that whatever journey we're on, we should take time to pay attention to the small, simple things in life, such as the beauty of flowers, the chatter of streams, the fresh smell of the earth in springtime, the caress of a breeze against our faces, and the taste of our favourite snack.

Enjoy flowers whenever you can

Often, when we think about journeys, we think about being on the move, "going places". Some people might think I'm not going anywhere much, since I can't move around as easily as most other cats, and since I have health challenges that might stick with me throughout my life.

But I can tell you for sure that I have many more journeys ahead of me, and this book is one of them. It's a new adventure for me and Mum, and we hope that by sharing my story with others, we can make new connections, deepen insights, create ties, form friendships, and spread love and understanding.

I'm just a little cat with mobility challenges. I don't think I'm more special than you are. Each of us is unique. Each of us has challenges and strengths. Some days are great. Other days are frustrating. I've come to understand that this is what it means to be alive — bravely facing whatever we need to face, and celebrating each happiness and success, small or big. I try to meet every day with a spirit of determination and openness. Sometimes, I burrow under a blanket and take a break from the challenges. Other times, I meet dragons and talk with hummingbirds and hang out with bats.

I'm happy and proud to be me. I hope, my friend, that you're happy and proud to be you.

With love,

~ Lua ~

The Road goes ever on and on
Down from the door where it began.
Now far ahead the Road has gone,
And I must follow, if I can,
Pursuing it with eager feet,
Until it joins some larger way,
Where many paths and errands meet.
And whither then? I cannot say.

— J.R.R. Tolkien, *The Fellowship of the Ring*

more information

The Book and Lua

You are very welcome to contact us!

Lua's email: thebookoflua@gmail.com
Dania's email: dania.sheldon@icloud.com

Facebook page for *The Book of Lua*: https://www.facebook.com/TheBookOfLua/
Facebook page for Lua: https://www.facebook.com/PrincipessaLua/

Videos of Lua

All of these videos were created by Douglas Brown using footage and stills provided by Sharon Samuels, Karen Duncan, and/or Dania, depending on the video:

Lua the Brave and Beautiful Kitten: https://www.youtube.com/watch?v=E_jn_TE9Hfo&t=11s
Lua the Brave and Beautiful Kitten – Part 2 – Lua's Progress: https://www.youtube.com/watch?v=RQXCCKW0h88
Lua the Brave and Beautiful Kitten's 1st Snowfall: https://www.youtube.com/watch?v=NpyN-7K3JhM
Lua the Snow Kitten: https://www.youtube.com/watch?v=5JGTmuo7zbo
A Visit With Lua the Kitten: https://www.youtube.com/watch?v=OReSh0ZVJds
I Are Cute Kitten Lua: https://www.youtube.com/watch?v=EoCw8ioXYfc
Lua the Brave and Beautiful Kitten Turns 1: https://www.youtube.com/watch?v=DUgYdybeeaw

Vancouver Orphan Kitten Rescue Association (VOKRA)

VOKRA's mission is to end cat overpopulation and homelessness. We rescue, heal, then place cats — first in our network of foster homes, then in carefully matched, loving, forever homes. We are a passionate, volunteer-driven charity with extensive cat care experience. We believe that no-kill is the only responsible approach, that trap-neuter-return works, and that cats are awesome.

Website: www.vokra.ca
Facebook: https://www.facebook.com/VOKRA/
Email: info@vokra.ca
Blog: http://vokrablog.ca
Twitter: http://twitter.com/VOKRAtweets
Instagram: https://www.instagram.com/vokra/
YouTube: http://www.youtube.com/user/VanOrphanKitten

Cats Alive Gabriola

Cats Alive Gabriola is a registered charitable organization whose purpose is to support and promote the welfare of cats on Gabriola Island through: spay/neutering; financially assisting low-income cat guardians; fostering homeless cats and matching them with caring humans; and feeding and providing medical care for neglected cats.

Facebook: https://www.facebook.com/groups/750673684960490/
Email: catsalivegabriola@gmail.com
Telephone: 1+250-816-2287

Tenth Life

Tenth Life saves stray cats and kittens in the St. Louis, Missouri, area, prioritizing those with special needs. They gave Dania invaluable advice when she first started caring for Lua, and they are a wealth of information and support about cats with special needs.

Tenth Life provides veterinary care, foster homes, and adoptive placement to stray cats and kittens, prioritizing those with special needs. They work to end unnecessary euthanasia and cat homelessness through educational outreach, community programs, and collaborative partnerships. Tenth Life believes that every cat, regardless of emotional or physical limitations, deserves the chance at a fulfilling and happy life. If a veterinarian determines that a cat is in a state of incurable suffering, Tenth Life relieves them of their pain through gentle and humane euthanasia. This decision is never made due to negative behaviours, a lack of space, or the difficulty or expense of a cat's medical needs.

Website: tenthlifecats.org
Facebook: https://www.facebook.com/tenthlifecats/?fref=ts

Cats With Paralysis and Mobility Challenges

This is a Facebook group providing discussion, advice, resources, and support for people who have cats with rear paralysis and other conditions that limit and/or challenge mobility (for example, cerebellar hypoplasia, twisted leg, amputations, congenital birth defects). Such conditions do not have to be a death sentence, even though many folks think they are. These cats can lead long, happy, and healthy lives with the proper care.

Facebook: https://www.facebook.com/groups/CatsWithParalysis/

credits

Pages 5 & 6, Lua and Bruce: Both images courtesy of Karen Duncan.
Page 7, Lua with paw raised: Image courtesy of Martin Godwyn.
Page 12, Lua on her back doing yoga: Image courtesy of Yasmin Abidi.
Page 19, Ravenscourt Park, London Underground sign: public domain.
Page 24, Lua as a kitten in the snow: Image courtesy of Martin Godwyn.
Page 27, Anna's Hummingbird: Image by Brocken Inaglory, CC BY-SA 3.0 (http://creativecommons.org/licenses/by-sa/3.0), via Wikimedia Commons.
Page 29, Close-up of Lua in the grass: Image courtesy of Martin Godwyn.
Page 30, Lion in Namibia: Image by Kevin Pluck (Flickr: The King.) CC BY 2.0 (http://creativecommons.org/licenses/by/2.0), via Wikimedia Commons.
Page 30, Lua being petted at the vet clinic: Image courtesy of Douglas Brown.
Page 37, Lua in her carrier at the vet clinic: Image courtesy of Douglas Brown.

Page 39, Lua receiving acupuncture and laser treatment: Three images courtesy of Douglas Brown.

Pages 44, 46, 47, 49, 51–55, 57, 80, 85, 86: All images courtesy of Martin Godwyn.

Page 48, Little Brown Bat cluster: Image by U.S. Fish and Wildlife Service Northeast Region (Little brown bat cluster), CC BY 2.0 (http://creativecommons.org/licenses/by/2.0) or public domain, via Wikimedia Commons.

Page 62, Mouse in the grass: Image courtesy of Martin Godwyn.

Page 63, Pedro, Stellar, and Bear: Both images courtesy of Martin Godwyn.

Page 64, Curly: Image courtesy of Martin Godwyn.

Page 66, Bruce outdoors and with his dad: Images courtesy of Diana Vileita.

Page 72, *Pipistrellus pipistrellus* bat on a thumb: Image by Gilles San Martin from Namur, Belgium, CC BY-SA 2.0 (http://creativecommons.org/licenses/by-sa/2.0), via Wikimedia Commons.

Page 81, *Aquilegia brevistyla*: Original painting by Mary Vaux Walcott. Internet Archive Book Images (No restrictions), via Wikimedia Commons.

Page 95, Excerpt from THE FELLOWSHIP OF THE RING by J.R.R. Tolkien. Copyright © 1954, 1965 by J.R.R. Tolkien. Copyright © renewed 1982 by Christopher R. Tolkien, Michael H.R. Tolkien, John F.R. Tolkien and Priscilla M.A.R. Tolkien. Used by permission of Houghton Mifflin Harcourt Publishing Company and by permission of HarperCollins Publishers Ltd. All rights reserved.

Page 102, Lua and her mum: Image courtesy of Seonaid Renwick.

about the authors

This is **Lua**'s first book, but she had so much fun creating it that she might write another. In the meantime, she will continue to befriend dragons, talk with ravens and hummingbirds, dig holes in The Mouse Garden, bask in front of the wood stove on cool days, lounge on The Magic Robe, and snuggle with her cat buddies and her mum.

Dania has been an editor since 1997, a writer since 2007, and a lover of cats and all other creatures, great and small, for as long as she can remember. She has also been a volunteer with Vancouver Orphan Kitten Rescue Association since 2005 and with Gabriola Cats Alive since 2009. When she is not providing meticulous service for her several cats, or working with clients, she tries to help the local wildlife and spends time with her family and friends.